OWN YOUR
IMPACT

GROWTH

PURPOSE

IMPACT

SUCCESS

Strategies for
Authors and Entrepreneurs
to Establish Authority and
Make a Lasting Impact

Juanita N. Woodson

OWN YOUR IMPACT

Strategies for Authors and Entrepreneurs to Establish Authority and Make a Lasting Impact

Juanita N. Woodson

Own Your Impact: Strategies for Authors and Entrepreneurs to Establish Authority and Make a Lasting Impact

Published by Grace 4 Purpose, Publishing Co. LLC

ISBN: 979-8-9926893-6-5

Book cover design by Grace 4 Purpose Publishing Co. LLC

Printed and bound in the United States of America

Table of Contents

INTRODUCTION:

Why Your Impact Matters

Your purpose is not just for you. If you have connected with me on social media, you will often see me share this message. It is a timeless reminder that your testimony, words and insight can help the lives of so many others. Your story is necessary. A mission that matters. And a voice the world needs to hear.

Whether you're an author with a message that could shift mindsets, or an entrepreneur building something meaningful from the ground up, your impact goes beyond sales, likes, or followers. It's about the lives you touch, the hearts you inspire, and the legacy you're creating each time you show up fully as yourself.

I know what it's like to sit with ideas that feel too big for the moment you're in. To question if your words, your gifts, your experience, your presence, really holds weight. But I've also learned that clarity comes when we commit to showing up. That confidence is built through bold, imperfect action. And that authority isn't something granted by others, it's the purpose God created you for and it's something you decide to own.

This book is for you, the author who wants to write with impact and build something beyond the pages. The entrepreneur who wants to be known for substance, not noise. The thought leader who's ready to stop playing small and start walking in full authority. If you're ready to show up, speak out, and stand tall in your calling, you're in the right place.

Inside these pages, you'll find real-world strategies, mindset shifts, and practical tools to help you:

- Clarify your message and mission
- Build visibility with authenticity
- Establish yourself as a trusted voice
- Create content, offers, and opportunities that reflect your purpose
- Make a lasting impact, without losing your soul in the process. Because listen, staying grounded in the foundation of your faith matters.

The world doesn't need another copy-paste brand. It needs *you*. Your story. Your truth. Your voice.

Let's begin the journey of owning your impact.

Own Your Impact

PART 1:

FOUNDATIONS OF INFLUENCE

Own Your Impact

Chapter One

Embracing Your Identity and Message

Before you market anything, your book, your business, your brand, you must first understand who you are at your core. Just as importantly, you must remember whose you are. God is the giver of purpose, and when you root your identity in Him, your message becomes more than just content, it becomes your calling.

Your identity and message are the heartbeat of your impact. When you truly own your story, align with your values, and operate from purpose instead of pressure, you unlock a level of influence that can't be manufactured. You become unstoppable.

Owning Your Story: The Foundation of Your Brand

Every author and entrepreneur has a story that shaped their voice. Maybe yours was formed through loss, healing, breakthrough, or transformation. For me, it began when I became a mother fresh out of high school. That chapter didn't stop me, it shaped me. It refined my resilience and awakened my purpose. It led me to working with other moms who have a story of their own and needed a safe space to feel like they are not alone.

For you, maybe your story started with a situation that was out of your control, and instead of letting it break you, you learned, grew, and flourished from it. Or maybe it was a moment when you saw something broken in the world and knew you were called to be a part of the solution.

Your story isn't a side note. It's the foundation of your brand.

We often think our audience wants polish, perfection, and performance. But what they really want is honesty. They want to see themselves in your story. They want to know that you didn't have all the answers but chose to show up anyway.

When you embrace your full story, even the messy middle, you give others permission to do the same. And that's when change happens.

Reflection Prompt: What moments in your journey shaped the message you share today?

_____

_____

_____

_____

_____

Identifying Your Core Message and Values

Clarity attracts. Confusion repels.

If you're going to make an impact, you need to be able to clearly articulate:

- Who you are
- What you stand for
- What you help others achieve or understand

Your **core message** is the consistent truth that flows through everything you create, your books, your conversations, your content, your offers. It's the anchor of your brand.

Your **values** are the guiding principles that shape how you show up. They help you stay aligned, build trust, and make decisions with confidence and integrity.

Take the time to define these. You're not just building a brand, you're building trust with the community that you build. And trust is built on clarity, consistency, and character.

Clarity Check:
- My core message is: _____
- The 3 values I want my brand to reflect are:

_____

Building from Purpose, Not Pressure

In a world that rewards hustle, it's easy to start building from pressure. Chasing trends. Comparing your journey to someone else's. Measuring success by metrics instead of meaning.

I refused to do what everyone else was doing on social just to appear "successful." Standing firm in my values, my morals, and my authentic purpose will always be number one for me when it comes to owning my impact. You won't see me dancing in my reels to promote my content because that's just not me.

It's important to stand firm in who you are when you're laying the foundation of your brand. What works for someone else may not work for you, and that's okay. Trust—your audience can tell when something feels forced.

But real, lasting impact isn't built on pressure. It's built on **purpose.**

Purpose will sustain you when progress feels slow. Purpose will remind you that what you're building matters.
Purpose will keep you aligned when the noise around you grows loud.

Pressure leads to burnout. Purpose leads to legacy.

The most magnetic leaders are not the flashiest. They are the most grounded. Grounded in their why. Grounded in their faith. Grounded in their assignment.

So pause and ask yourself:
• Am I building from peace or from pressure?
• Do my actions reflect my mission or my insecurities?
• What would it look like to lead from a place of purpose?

You don't need to have it all figured out. You just need to be anchored in who you are and what you're called to do. Everything else flows from there.

Action Steps

1. Reflect on the Story That Shaped You
Take 10–15 minutes of quiet time to reflect on the moments—both joyful and painful—that helped shape your message. Journal one experience that grew your voice or clarified your purpose. Don't edit it for perfection—honor it for the growth it represents. This becomes a foundational piece of the message you carry.

2. Define Your Message and Values with Intention
Complete the clarity check in this chapter and prayerfully review your responses. Ask God to confirm your core message and highlight the values that should lead your brand. Once defined, post them somewhere visible in your creative space to serve as a daily reminder of your divine assignment.

3. Release the Pressure, Reclaim the Purpose
Make a bold decision today: identify one way you've been building from pressure (comparison, overworking, people-pleasing) and take one small action to shift back into purpose. Whether it's adjusting your schedule, unfollowing a distracting account, or taking a Sabbath rest—honor the calling, not the crowd.

Affirmation:

I am enough. My story is powerful. My purpose is clear. I am building from truth, not trends.

Own Your Impact

Chapter Two:

Overcoming Imposter Syndrome

You've got the vision. You've got the calling. But deep down, there's that quiet voice asking:

"Who do you think you are?"

Sound familiar?

That's imposter syndrome, sneaky, persistent, and always showing up right when you're about to step into something bold, meaningful, and outside your comfort zone. It whispers doubts, feeds your fears, and tries to convince you that you're not ready, not qualified, not "enough."

For years, I wrestled with it in silence. Opportunities I had prayed for would come my way, and instead of confidently saying yes, I hesitated. I minimized my gifts. I delayed taking action. Not because I didn't care, but because deep down, I questioned whether I truly belonged in the room or deserved a seat at the table.

There were moments I convinced myself that someone else could do it better. That I needed "more" before I could begin, more credentials, more experience, more approval. But what I really needed was to believe what God had already spoken about me.

Over the years, I've worked with many authors who struggled with the same fear. Before they ever published a book, they wondered if their voices mattered. They'd ask, *"Who's going to read my story?" "What if no one listens?"* And I understood, because I've been there too.

One of the biggest lies imposter syndrome has tried to sell me is this: *"You're doing too much."* And for a long time, I believed it. So I would shrink. I would shut down. I would silence parts of myself to fit into a box that wasn't even mine to begin with.

But not anymore.

Let's call it out. Let's cancel it. You are *not* doing too much. You are showing up in alignment with the assignment on your life.

Common Mindset Blocks (and How to Break Through)

You're not alone. Authors, entrepreneurs, speakers, and yes, even those with bestsellers and booked-out brands battle these same thoughts:

- *"I'm not an expert."*
- *"What if no one cares what I have to say?"*
- *"I don't have the credentials."*
- *"Others are doing it better."*

Here's the truth: Impact is not reserved for the perfect, the polished, or the popular. It's for the *willing*.

To overcome these mindset blocks:

1. **Recognize the lies** – Imposter syndrome thrives in silence. Speak your fears out loud and challenge them with truth.

2. **Reframe your perspective** – You're not here because you know *everything*—you're here because you've *lived something.*
3. **Take aligned action** – Confidence comes from doing. You silence doubt by doing the very thing it told you not to do.

Truth Reminder: You don't need permission to walk in your purpose.

The Comparison Trap

Comparison is one of the quickest ways to shrink your impact. If you have ever heard the saying, "comparison is the thief of joy". It is so true, it will have you second guessing your hard work and all the effort that you have put in. Comparison will have you afraid to walk into certain rooms or to use your voice because you feel it doesn't fit what everyone else is doing.

Scrolling social media or watching others rise can lead you to believe you're behind. But here's the reality: You're not behind, you're on *your* path. And your path is not meant to look like anyone else's.

Instead of comparing:

- **Celebrate others without questioning yourself**
- **Stay in your lane**—consistency over comparison
- **Use what you admire as inspiration, not intimidation**

What God has for *you* is still on schedule. Keep showing up.

Pause and Reflect: Who or what have you been comparing yourself to, and how can you shift your focus back to your mission?

Faith, Confidence, and Inner Authority

Imposter syndrome can't survive where *faith* lives.

Faith reminds you that your calling didn't come from you, it came through you. That means you're already equipped. Your confidence doesn't have to be built on your résumé, your title, or your metrics. It can be built on your faith, your consistency, and your willingness to grow.

Inner authority is when you stop looking outward for validation and start listening inward, to the truth God placed inside of you.

Confidence Confession:
I may not have all the answers, but I have the assignment.
I was called for this. I am ready. I will show up.

Action Step:
Write down 3 lies imposter syndrome has told you—and replace them with truth.

Example:

- *Lie:* "I'm not experienced enough."
- *Truth:* "My lived experience is more powerful than a title."

Next up, we'll talk about how to position yourself with purpose so that your message is clear, and your impact is intentional.

Affirmation:

I was called for this. I am ready. I will show up.

Chapter Three:

Positioning Yourself with Purpose

"Write the vision, and make it plain on tablets, so he may run who reads it." — Habakkuk 2:2 (ESV)

Purpose is powerful, but purpose with strategy is what positions you to truly make an impact.

Habakkuk 2:2 reminds us that vision isn't just for dreaming, it's for clarity, movement, and execution. When you write the vision plainly, you give yourself (and others) a path to follow. This chapter is designed to help you do just that: get clear, get focused, and move with intention.

If you're going to stand out in a crowded space, you have to be clear on:
• Who you serve
• What you bring to the table
• Why it matters

This chapter will help you define your niche, articulate your value, and step into your role with clarity, whether you're an author, entrepreneur, or a little bit of both.

Niche Clarity for Maximum Impact

Let's be honest, trying to serve everybody will drain you and confuse your audience. It leads to wasted time and unnecessary spending. I started to notice a shift when I got clear about my niche.

When I first began my journey as an author coach and publisher, I truly wanted to help everybody write and publish books. I meant well, but I made a few mistakes and took on some projects that didn't really align with my vision or what I believed in.

Some of those projects came my way because they were willing to pay, and at the time, my business needed the income. I was still growing, and let's be real, entrepreneurship is not for the weak. Whew.

But what I learned is this—just because someone is paying you doesn't mean you're making a profit. Some of those projects cost me more than money. They cost me peace of mind.

The game changed when I got clear on my niche, and I stood ten toes down behind it. When you know who you're called to serve and the problem you're called to help solve, your message becomes more magnetic. You're no longer shouting into the void. You're speaking directly to the people who need you the most.

Ask yourself:
• Who is my message, book, or brand really for?
• What problem am I helping them solve?
• Why am I passionate about helping this group?

Clarity attracts. And when your audience feels seen, they lean in.

Clarity Check-In:
I serve: _____
I help them: _____
So they can: _____

Defining Your Unique Value Proposition

Your **unique value proposition (UVP)** is what makes *you* different. It's the specific way you help people achieve transformation, growth, or breakthrough.

To define yours, consider:

- What perspective or lived experience do I bring?
- What results have I helped others achieve?
- What makes my approach, message, or offer stand out?

Whether you're writing books or launching programs, your UVP helps you rise above the noise and attract people who *value what you uniquely carry.*

Example UVP for an Author:

"I help women navigate healing, accept personal accountability, and faith after heartbreak through raw storytelling, biblical encouragement, and practical guidance."

Author vs. Entrepreneur: Understanding Your Role(s)

This part is key. Many people get stuck because they don't know how to *own both identities*, but you don't have to choose.

➡️ **As an author**, you're a storyteller, message-bearer, and legacy builder. Your role is to create content that connects, heals, or inspires.

➡ **As an entrepreneur**, you're a problem-solver, brand-builder, and impact generator. Your role is to package your message into offers, solutions, or services that serve your audience.

Knowing when you're operating as one or the other—or both—will help you make clearer decisions, set better goals, and build from a place of alignment, not confusion.

Quick Shift: Think like a writer when creating, think like an entrepreneur when sharing.
You don't just write, you *lead*.

Action Steps:

1. Define your niche in one sentence.
2. Write out your unique value proposition.
3. Identify which "hat" you're wearing in your current season—author, entrepreneur, or both—and how you can lead more intentionally from that space.

Next Up: We're diving into building your platform, because once you know your message and position, it's time to get visible and start building authority the right way.

Affirmation:

I know who I serve, what I carry, and why it matters.

My voice is necessary. My impact is intentional.

PART 2:

STRATEGIES TO ESTABLISH AUTHORITY

Own Your Impact

Chapter Four:

Build a Presence That Aligns With Your Purpose

You don't need a big platform. You need a meaningful one.
You don't have to be everywhere to make a difference.

One thing I had to learn on this journey is that your no is just as important as your yes. Earlier I shared how imposter syndrome made me shrink. Sometimes that looked like backing away from opportunities. But I had to learn to use wisdom and know the difference between imposter syndrome and when I truly needed to say no.

Every opportunity is not your assignment. Just because something looks good doesn't mean it is good for your purpose. Sometimes we can get so caught up in building a big platform that we end up out of alignment with God. And there is no good impact in that.

You just need to show up where it counts. With a message that is clear, consistent, and true to who you are.

Your platform is not just a place to post content. It is an extension of your voice. It is where people experience the heart of your message before they ever buy your book, register for your class, or book a session.

Let's make sure what they experience speaks for you, even when you are not in the room.

Choose Presence Over Pressure

Not every platform is for you, and that's okay. One of the biggest lessons I learned is to track where the engagement happens the most.

Instead of chasing trends, let's build from a place of alignment. Choose platforms that:

- Match how you naturally communicate
- Allow space for real connection
- Help your message land where it's needed most

Here are a few places to consider:

- **Website** – This is your digital home. A space to house your story, your services, your next steps. It doesn't need to be fancy—but it should reflect *you*.
- **Instagram / Threads / LinkedIn / Facebook** – Choose one or two. Don't stretch yourself thin. Focus on where your audience is and where you enjoy showing up.
- **Podcast or YouTube** – If your voice or presence makes the message stronger, this could be your lane. But only if it feels sustainable.
- **Email List** – This is sacred. A direct line to your people. If you're going to pour into any platform— make it this one.

Ask this instead of "Where should I be?" → "Where can I show up with purpose and stay consistent?"

Show Up With Meaning, Not Just Content

You don't need to be loud to be effective.
You just need to offer something that *helps*.

Instead of trying to "create content," focus on offering real value:

- **Educate** – Share what you've learned through experience
- **Encourage** – Remind them they're not alone
- **Empower** – Give them tools or clarity to take a step forward

Here are some content ideas that feel natural and honest:

- Moments from your journey: what you're learning, what you're letting go
- Client wins or lessons learned from coaching sessions
- Practical advice for writers, dreamers, or purpose-driven women
- Personal reflections that connect back to your message or faith
- Invitations: "Here's how we can walk together"

You don't have to post every day. You just have to show up with something *real*.

Let Your Brand Look and Sound Like You

You don't need a marketing degree to show up well online. You just need to be intentional.

Visuals matter—here's how to keep it simple:

- Pick 2–3 brand colors that feel aligned with your message
- Use 1–2 fonts to keep things clean and cohesive
- Invest in a good headshot or take a clear, natural photo
- Use branded templates for consistency (Canva is your friend)

Now let's talk voice:

- Are you calm and grounded? Warm and honest? Bold and faith-filled? Let that guide how you write.
- Talk to one person. Not the crowd. Speak as if you're writing to the woman you were called to serve.
- Keep it clear, purposeful, and personal. That's what builds trust.

Your brand voice isn't just how you sound, it's how you make people feel.

Action Steps

1. **Pick 1–2 platforms** you'll show up on for the next 90 days—consistently and with intention.
2. **Define your 3 content pillars.** What are the main themes you want to be known for? (e.g. Faith & Writing, Life Coaching for Women, Owning Your Voice)
3. **Do a quick brand check.** Does your visual presence reflect your message, values, and current direction?

Next Up: In the next chapter, we'll talk about increasing your visibility, but in a way that doesn't compromise your authenticity.

Affirmation:

I choose presence over pressure.
My platform reflects my purpose, not my ego.
I don't chase trends—I build with intention.
Every space I show up in honors who I am and who I'm called to serve.
I don't have to be everywhere—just where it counts.

Chapter Five:

Writing with Purpose, Not Performance

Writing isn't just about producing content. It's about producing change.

Whether you're working on your next book, sharing a personal story online, or sending an email to your community, your words carry weight.

They don't need to be loud to be powerful. They just need to be intentional.

Your voice can:
• Offer hope
• Create connection
• Teach truth
• Spark transformation

This chapter is about helping you write from your core message, not for the algorithm, so your words carry the influence they were meant to.

Write to Serve, Not to Impress

Your words should do more than take up space. They should meet someone right where they are.

If your writing starts to feel heavy, forced, or disconnected, it might be because the focus has shifted. Maybe it became more about sounding impressive than being helpful. The truth is people aren't looking for perfection. They are looking for real answers, relatable insight, and honest encouragement.

They want to know what you've struggled with and how you overcame it. So often we try to present ourselves as experts without evidence. But your impact is found in your authenticity, not your performance.

Before you jump into your next chapter, caption, blog post, or email, pause and ask yourself:

- **Who am I writing this for?**
  Visualize one person. Not your whole audience. Just one. What are they navigating today? What's weighing on them? What do they need to hear, not to be wowed, but to feel supported, seen, and less alone?
- **What are they walking through right now?**
  Get in the thick of it with them. Maybe they're trying to finish a project, start a business, process something heavy, or just hold it together. When your words meet people in their real-life moments, that's when they stick.
- **How can my words offer clarity, courage, or next steps?**
  You don't have to have all the answers. But can your words help them breathe deeper? Think differently? Take one step forward? That's what writing with impact looks like, it helps people move, even in the smallest ways.

Here's the thing: writing to impress puts the focus on you. Writing to serve puts the focus where it belongs, on the person you're called to help.

You're not here to perform. You're here to pour into others with the experiences, lessons, and insight you've gained along the way.

Because when you write from a place of care, purpose, and truth, your words don't just sound good, they *do good.*

Your Story is More Than a Testimony: It's a Tool

People don't connect to perfect. They connect to real.

At one point in my journey as an author and entrepreneur, I tried to tuck away parts of my story. Not out of fear, but because I thought, "That season has passed. Do I really need to keep bringing that up?" I tried to hide the parts where I failed, the seasons where I didn't see progress. There were even parts of my story that I simply did not want to share anymore because I had healed through those moments.

But what I came to understand is this: purpose doesn't expire. And your story doesn't stop working just because you've moved on.

The truth is, someone is walking through what you've already overcome. Your willingness to share it, honestly and with intention, can give them the courage to keep going. That makes your story more than a testimony. It makes it a tool.

Not a tool for performance. Not for validation or applause. A tool for building connection, trust, and hope.

When you own your journey, your struggles, your pivots, your process, you give others permission to do the same.

Remember, your purpose is not just for you.

Here's what storytelling like that does:

- **It builds trust.** People lean in when they know you've lived what you're teaching.
- **It makes your message more relatable.** It's not just theory, it's lived experience.
- **It shows what's possible.** You're proof that hard seasons don't have the final say.

A Storytelling Rhythm That Works

If you're not sure how to shape your story, try this rhythm:

Struggle → Shift → Solution

1. **Struggle** – Start with a real moment. What were you up against? What season tested you? What did it feel like to be in it?
2. **Shift** – What changed? Maybe it was a moment of clarity, a conversation, or a decision that helped you see things differently.
3. **Solution** – What helped you grow? What did you learn, gain, or walk away with that someone else might need?

You don't need to air everything. You're not required to be an open book. But you *are* equipped to be a helpful one.

Just share enough for someone to see themselves in your journey, and enough truth to let them know change is possible for them, too.

Because your story isn't just about where you've been, it's a reminder of what's possible when purpose leads the way.

Write Like a Leader, Even Without the Title

You don't need a platform of thousands to be a thought leader. You just need to lead with thoughtfulness.

When your words carry conviction, clarity, and compassion, they start conversations that last beyond the scroll.

Ask yourself:

- What am I called to say that others might be afraid to?
- What values or truths do I want to keep centering?
- What do I want my words to leave behind in someone's heart?

Your writing doesn't need to go viral to matter. It just needs to move the *right people*.

Action Steps

1. **Choose a story** from your life or journey that connects to your core message. Write it out using the *Struggle–Shift–Solution* framework.
2. **Identify 2–3 themes** you want to be known for (e.g., faith in hard seasons, writing through healing, building purpose-driven platforms).
3. **Reflect on your content.** Is it rooted in information, transformation—or both? Where can you lean in deeper?

Next Up: Now that your message is anchored in clarity and your writing flows with intention, it's time to talk visibility. But not the kind that drains you or makes you perform. We're going to explore how to *be seen* without losing yourself in the process.

Affirmation:

Every story I share is a tool, not a show.
I write to serve, connect, and move others
forward—one honest word at a time.

Chapter Six:

Speaking and Teaching as a Growth Strategy

Writing opens the door, but speaking is what puts you in the room.

Whether you are on a stage, teaching a workshop, hosting a webinar, or leading a panel, your voice carries weight when it is shared with intention and confidence.

Speaking and teaching are more than just visibility tools. They are impact multipliers. They help your message reach further, connect deeper, and create lasting transformation beyond the page.

But you have to do the work to become visible. If you want to be seen as an authority in your niche, if you want to be someone people remember to call on for certain topics, you have to show up with consistency and purpose.

You have to make that decision first. Decide if this is the path you are supposed to walk down before you continue. Because once you do, your voice becomes part of how you lead.

Why Every Author and Entrepreneur Should Speak

If you have a message, you have a reason to speak.

Speaking:

- Builds trust and credibility faster than almost anything else

- Allows your audience to connect with your energy and authenticity
- Opens doors to partnerships, clients, and media opportunities
- Turns your message into a movement

For authors, speaking turns your book into a *business.* For entrepreneurs, it turns your expertise into *influence.*

Reminder: You don't have to be perfect to be powerful. Speak from your story, and your audience will lean in. Your voice does not need to sound like everyone else's to make an impact.

Structuring Signature Talks, Workshops, and Webinars

Your message deserves structure, not just passion.

Think back to a time when you were listening to someone speak and you couldn't keep up with what they were saying. They jumped from topic to topic, shared stories that didn't connect, and by the end, you were confused instead of inspired. You left with nothing.

We are going to avoid that.

Over the years, I have had multiple opportunities to speak. Listen, I am a PK, so it was going to happen whether I wanted to or not. Before I ever became an entrepreneur or wrote my first book, I was speaking in front of people. And let me tell you, I did not like it.

But one thing that experience taught me was how to structure my messages. That foundation helped me more than I realized. And it definitely helps that we are authors. We already know how to structure blogs, chapters, and books.

As my brand grew and I started writing more books, I began to position myself in front of the right audience. That led to even more opportunities to share my testimony and teach people what I have learned through my journey in entrepreneurship and publishing.

Now if I'm being honest, I can't say the nervousness of speaking in front of people has completely gone away. It hasn't. But that's because it's not about me. I am always prayerful that what I deliver stays aligned with what God wants me to say.

Let's breakdown what that looks like:

Signature Talk (20–60 min)

- **Hook** – Start with a relatable story, stat, or question
- **Heart** – Share your journey or expertise in a way that resonates
- **Help** – Offer practical takeaways your audience can use right away
- **Invitation** – End with a clear call to action (buy the book, visit your site, join your email list, etc.)

Workshop

- Interactive, educational, and packed with value
- Outline your main teaching points
- Add moments for reflection, breakout activities, or Q&A

- Provide a workbook or worksheet when possible

Webinar

- Similar to a workshop but typically ends with an offer (book, service, program)
- Be sure it educates before it sells
- Keep it conversational and focused on outcomes for the audience

Pro Tip: Practice until it feels like a conversation, not a performance.

Virtual vs. In-Person Opportunities

Both are valuable, and both can expand your reach.

Virtual Speaking (Zoom, podcasts, summits)

- Great for accessibility and global reach
- Easier to land for beginners
- Can be recorded and repurposed for future content

In-Person Speaking (conferences, churches, schools, events)

- Deepens connection and trust instantly
- Often leads to more powerful referrals and networking
- Allows you to sell your book or services on the spot

Start where you are. You don't need a TEDx stage— start with your circle, your community, or your email list.

Your first "stage" might be a podcast or a local library event.

Action Steps:

1. Draft an outline for a signature talk that connects to your book, business, or personal story.
2. Choose one virtual or in-person speaking opportunity to pursue within the next 30 days.
3. Record yourself speaking for 3–5 minutes to begin refining your delivery.

Next Up: In the next chapter, we'll unpack visibility strategies to help you reach new audiences and consistently show up with impact—without burning out or blending in.

Affirmation:

Every time I teach, I build trust, shift perspectives, and serve well.

Chapter Seven:

Media, PR, and Podcasting

You've done the deep work.
You've written the book, refined your message, and embraced your voice.

We have worked through the imposter syndrome.
We know when to say yes and when to say no.
You've done the work. Now it is time to show up.

It's time to step beyond the pages and into the spotlight. Visibility isn't about ego. It's about access. It's about creating the kind of presence that allows your message to reach the people it was meant to serve.

It's strategy, not self-promotion.

This chapter is your invitation to show up with boldness and brilliance. So opportunities don't just pass you by. They stop right at your door.

Getting Featured: How to Pitch Yourself

Media doesn't always knock first. Sometimes you have to knock for it.

Here's a truth most people overlook—media outlets, blogs, podcasts, and digital shows are always looking for fresh voices and relevant content. Your story, your insight, your expertise could be exactly what they are looking for.

The key is knowing how to position yourself.

When I first got started, I began with what was accessible to me. I reached out to my local library when I launched my first book. That small step led to my book being placed in a public library, and it also opened the door for my photo and story to be featured in our local newspaper.

Visibility takes intention and effort. I did not wait for opportunities to be handed to me. I showed up, introduced myself, and shared my message.

Your next media opportunity may not come from a major outlet right away, but every open door counts. The more you position yourself with clarity and purpose, the more doors will open.

To pitch with purpose:

- **Lead with relevance.** Tie your message into something current, whether it's a trending topic, an upcoming awareness month, or a cultural conversation.
- **Be clear and concise.** Introduce yourself quickly. Share what you do, why you're credible, and how you'll serve their audience.
- **Use credibility markers.** Mention your book, speaking engagements, previous features, or social reach to establish trust and authority.
- **Make it easy to say yes.** Include a brief bio, a professional headshot, social media links, and a few sample topics you can speak on with confidence.

Example Pitch Structure:

- Hook or connection point (Why them? Why now?)
- Quick bio
- Why your topic matters to their audience
- What listeners or readers will walk away with
- Clear call-to-action (Ex: "I'd love to connect for an interview—let me know if we can set up a time!")

Reminder: You don't have to wait to be discovered. You can *position* yourself to be seen.

Becoming a Sought-After Guest

Landing one feature is great—but becoming the guest people invite back and recommend to others? That's real impact.

You don't need to overthink it, but you do need to be intentional. When you show up with the right energy and preparation, you stand out—in the best way.

Here's how to be the guest they remember:

- **Do your homework.** Take time to learn about the show, the host, and their audience. What do they care about? What topics do they usually cover? Show them you're not just showing up to talk, you're showing up to serve.
- **Serve before you sell.** Don't make it all about your book or your brand. Share something helpful. Give a takeaway the audience can actually use. That's what keeps people engaged, and makes hosts want to have you back.
- **Know your signature message.** Be clear about what you're known for and keep repeating it. When your message is consistent, it becomes

memorable—and that's what builds recognition over time.

- **Share the spotlight.** When the episode goes live, post it. Tag the host. Talk about it. The more you share it, the more visibility you create—for both of you. And trust me, hosts notice that.

⌄ **Pro Tip:** Podcast interviews live *forever*. That one conversation can keep working for you—months or even years later—bringing new people into your world.

When I published my first book, I made it clear that I wanted to get my message out. I talked about it on social media, in conversations, and anywhere I could. The more I shared, the more people started reaching out, inviting me onto podcasts and radio interviews. Opportunities didn't just show up out of nowhere, I positioned myself to be seen and heard.

You don't have to wait for someone to discover you. Be the one who shows up, and makes it easy to say yes.

Launching Your Own Podcast for Long-Term Credibility

Hosting your own podcast isn't just trendy. It's powerful.

Why?
• It positions you as a thought leader
• It gives you consistent content for your brand
• It allows you to create community and connection
• It opens the door to collaborations and interviews with others in your field

Start simple:
• Choose a clear theme tied to your brand or message
• Outline 5 to 10 episode ideas to begin
• Record your intro, outro, and first 2 to 3 episodes
• Publish on platforms like Spotify, Apple, or YouTube

Podcast Tip: You don't need fancy equipment. You need good content and consistency. That's what builds trust and credibility over time.

Action Steps:

1. Write a short media pitch using the template above and send it to one podcast, blog, or outlet this week.
2. Identify 3 shows or platforms your target audience listens to and start engaging with their content.
3. Brainstorm a potential podcast name and theme— just for fun (or the future!).

Next Up: Now that you know how to be seen and heard in the media, we'll wrap up with strategies for *sustaining your impact*—because consistency is the secret sauce to long-term influence.

Affirmation:

My message is valuable, my story is needed,
and my voice belongs in the room.

PART 3:

BUILDING A BUSINESS AROUND YOUR IMPACT

Chapter 8:

Creating Offers That Align with Your Mission

Impact and income can co-exist beautifully when your offers are built with intention.

When your work is grounded in purpose, when it's tied to your story, your mission, and a desire to serve; sales don't feel like selling. They feel like invitations into transformation. That's what it's really about.

In this chapter, we're talking about how to build books, coaching programs, courses, and communities that help you serve, lead, and earn, without compromising your voice or values.

Your Message Deserves Multiple Rooms

You weren't meant to keep your message in one box. One book, one product, one post? That's just the beginning. When you allow your message to evolve into offers that meet people where they are, you multiply your impact.

Let me share how this unfolded for me.

When I launched *The Authors Impact Hub*, it wasn't just about creating another space, it was about giving authors real support. Not just encouragement, but **tools, tips, and strategy** they could use to grow. I wanted to create a space where authors didn't feel lost in the noise. A space where they could learn, share, and thrive.

It didn't stop there.

53

From a collaborative book project came the *Moments for Moms* community, proof that books don't just end when the last page is written. That project brought together women with powerful stories, and from that unity grew something deeper: a space for moms to feel seen, supported, and spiritually grounded. The book was the seed. The community became the garden.

Formats That Can Carry Your Message

Whether you're just starting or expanding your reach, here are four powerful ways to package what you offer:

Books

- Your foundation—it builds credibility and makes your message visible.
- Opens doors to speaking, workshops, curriculum, and partnerships.
- Can lead to deeper relationships with your audience.

Coaching

- One-on-one or group mentorship that provides clarity, guidance, and transformation.
- Ideal for service-based entrepreneurs and storytellers with lived wisdom.
- Helps people implement, not just consume.

Courses

- A great way to turn your process into a step-by-step path others can follow.

- Allows your audience to work through your content at their own pace (or with live support).
- Scalable and sustainable.

Communities / Memberships

- This is where long-term connection and transformation happen.
- Whether it's an author circle, a monthly devotional space, or a resource hub, community brings your work to life.
- Recurring revenue, deeper engagement, and an opportunity to lead ongoing conversations.

Ask yourself: *What would someone need next after they read my book or heard me speak?* Build that.

Pricing That Honors Your Work

Let's talk about money, with confidence.

Your pricing should reflect the **transformation you provide**, not just the time it takes to deliver it. It's not about attaching your worth to a number, it's about making **aligned, sustainable decisions** that let you serve well *without burning out.*

When I first started out, I honestly wasn't sure what to charge. I just knew I wanted to help people—especially first-time authors get their books out into the world. I'd been through the process myself, and I knew how confusing and overwhelming it could be. So I undercharged. A lot. I told myself I was just "getting started," or that I didn't want to scare people away with my prices.

But over time, I realized something: **undervaluing my work didn't serve anyone, not me, and not my clients**.

Here's the truth no one tells you early on:
Cheap clients often bring the most problems. They're more likely to second-guess your expertise, push boundaries, or expect high-level transformation on a low-level commitment. Why? Because they're not truly invested. And when people aren't invested, they rarely implement.

I had to overcome the fear of setting my price—and be willing to **stand firm in it**. That took time, growth, and a mindset shift. But it changed everything.

Now, I price my offers based on:

- The **value** and **results** they provide
- The **time, energy, and access** involved
- My **long-term goals**, boundaries, and capacity
- The **life I'm called to build**, not just the business I'm running

Quick Tip: Don't just list features. Instead of saying "8 modules" or "3 calls," highlight the shift. *What's different in someone's life after working with you or reading your book?* That's the transformation people are really paying for.

When you anchor your price in **impact**, it becomes easier to communicate it with confidence, and attract the people who are ready, willing, and grateful to grow with you.

And let me say this: you are allowed to grow. Your pricing is allowed to evolve as you do. Just make sure it always reflects the value, not your doubt.

Monetizing Without Compromising

You don't have to sell like everyone else to succeed.
You can build a profitable brand that's **honest, heartfelt, and deeply impactful.**
You can lead with integrity, stay true to your mission, and still get paid well for the transformation you provide.

Here's how to do that:

Lead with purpose.

You're not here to push people, you're here to *serve* them.
When your heart is in the right place, it shows. People can feel when your intention is genuine. It's not about perfect sales scripts or fancy funnels, it's about being clear on *why* your offer exists in the first place.
Ask yourself: *How does this help someone move forward? What problem does this solve?* That's the foundation of purpose-driven marketing.

Focus on relationships.

Behind every email, like, or comment is a real person. Talk to them like you would if they were sitting across from you at the kitchen table. Let them know you see them, hear them, and care about their journey.
Because when people feel seen, they trust you. And trust is the real currency of any lasting business.

When I launched the **Authors Impact Hub**, I didn't come in with a sales agenda, I came in with a *service mindset.* I wanted to create a space where authors felt supported, equipped, and celebrated. The same with the **Moments for Moms: Legacy Unlocked** community. That space was birthed out of a book collaboration, but it became so much more because I focused on connection, not conversion.

Offer solutions.

Don't just market your product, **communicate the change it will bring**.
How does your offer make life better, simpler, or more hopeful for someone else?
When you show up to help, instead of just sell, people lean in. You're not just asking them to buy, you're offering them a way forward.

Instead of saying, "Buy my course," say, "Here's how this course helps you finally finish that book you've been dreaming about."

Let your story guide your strategy.

What you've lived through, that's your edge. That's your credibility.
People are drawn to authenticity, and your lived experience is what makes your message resonate. You don't have to pretend to be further ahead than you are. You don't need a perfect past, you just need to be real. Use your story to help someone else take the next step in theirs.

You don't need to be louder. You just need to be **clearer**. About **who you help**, **how you help**, and **why it matters.**

When your message is aligned, your marketing becomes an invitation, not a pitch.

Action Steps

1. Choose **one offer** (book, course, service, or membership) to refine, launch, or promote within the next 30 days.
2. Clearly outline the **transformation** it offers— what shifts when someone says yes?
3. Set a **price** that aligns with your energy, impact, and income goals.

Next Up:

You've built offers with purpose, now it's time to focus on building your *people*. In the next chapter, we'll talk about growing authentic connections and creating a loyal audience that walks with you for the long haul.

Affirmation:

I serve from my story, price with confidence, and lead with heart.
My work is valuable, my voice is needed, and I am worthy of building a life that reflects both.

Chapter Nine:

Growth with Grace

You can grow your brand without grinding yourself into the ground.

Showing up consistently builds trust, but consistency doesn't mean chaos, and it certainly doesn't mean burnout.
You don't need to do everything. You just need to focus on the *right* things, do them with intention, and build systems that support you as you grow.

This chapter is about giving structure to your calling, space for your creativity, and grace for your journey.

Email Marketing Made Simple (and Soulful)

Your email list is *not* just a marketing tool—it's a ministry, a conversation, and a direct connection to your audience. Social media may be where you wave hello, but email is where you sit down and *talk*. It's space you own. And it's one of your most powerful ways to nurture trust and build community.

Here's how to make it simple, soulful, and strategic:

1. Start with a Lead Magnet That Solves a Real Problem

Think small, specific, and helpful.
It doesn't need to be fancy—it just needs to *serve*. A checklist, devotional, mini-guide, video tutorial, or even a free template works well if it addresses one need your

ideal reader has.

Ask yourself: *What's one thing I can help them do or understand faster, easier, or with more clarity?*

2. Create a Warm Welcome Sequence

This is where your new subscriber meets the real you. Automate 3–5 emails that gently introduce your story, your values, and how you can help them move forward. Invite them in like family, not followers.

A simple flow:

- **Email 1:** Welcome and your "why"
- **Email 2:** Share a quick win or tip
- **Email 3:** Your offer or community
- **Email 4:** Personal story or testimony
- **Email 5:** Invitation to connect further (free call, resource, or group)

3. Email Consistently

You don't need to email daily, but you *do* need to show up regularly.

Weekly or biweekly is a good rhythm. Treat it like a check-in, not a broadcast. Share tips, behind-the-scenes moments, or lessons you're learning.

Be real. Be generous. Be consistent.

Pro Tip: Focus on *value first*, sales second.

People should feel like opening your email is a gift, not a grab. Create a space that feels like conversation, not a constant pitch.

Automation Tools and Time Management That Serve You

You don't have to juggle everything alone.

Automation is not about losing your personal touch. It is about protecting your energy and keeping your business flowing even when life gets busy.

Let systems do the heavy lifting so you can stay focused on the mission.

For me, sometimes I need to step away from everything. Social media, emails, and even the creative work. I need space to rest, recharge, and realign. Having the right systems in place allows me to do that without everything falling apart.

You can still show up for your audience and run your business well, even while taking care of yourself. That is the power of automation and time management that actually works for you.

Automation Tools and Time Management Tips

You're one person, but automation helps you move like a team.

Some tools to streamline your systems:

- **Email Platforms:** MailerLite, ConvertKit, Flodesk
- **Content Scheduling:** Planoly, Later, Buffer, and **Canva**

- ○ Canva isn't just for design anymore, it now lets you schedule social media posts directly from the platform. This means you can create your graphics and plan your posting calendar all in one place, saving you time and keeping things organized.
- ○ **Tips for using Canva scheduling:**
  - ▪ Batch-create your content ahead of time, then schedule posts for days or weeks in advance.
  - ▪ Use Canva's calendar view to get a visual overview of your planned content.
  - ▪ Take advantage of Canva's ability to post across multiple platforms like Instagram, Facebook, Twitter, LinkedIn, and Pinterest.
  - ▪ Set reminders for timely posts or special events.
- **Client & Course Management:** Honeybook (my go-to for CRM and automation—user-friendly and easy to set up). I especially use it to automate challenge sign-ups, payments, and follow-ups.
  - ○ For a less expensive alternative, consider **Dubsado** or **17hats**—both offer solid CRM and automation features with flexible pricing.
- **Calendars & Workflows:** Google Calendar, Trello, Notion, ClickUp

Time Management Tips:

- Batch your content. Record or write multiple pieces of content at once to save time.

- Theme your days. Assign specific days for admin, content creation, client calls, etc.
- Use templates. Reuse and repurpose content across platforms and formats.

Automation doesn't take away your authenticity, it amplifies your message without draining your energy.

Collaborations and Partnerships That Align with Purpose

You don't have to grow alone.

Some of your biggest breakthroughs will come through partnerships rooted in shared mission, aligned values, and mutual respect.

When I launched the **Authors Impact Hub**, I knew I wasn't building just another brand, I was building a *movement*. I wanted to create a space where authors could access the tools, guidance, and support they needed to thrive. But even more than that, I wanted to build a **community**, one that championed each other's wins, learned through shared experiences, and cultivated real impact.

That same desire birthed the **Moments for Moms** community. What started as a simple book collaboration grew into something far more meaningful, a space for women to be seen, heard, and empowered by each other's stories. That evolution didn't happen in isolation. It happened because I *leaned into collaboration*. I invited others to the table, amplified their gifts, and built trust-based relationships that helped all of us rise together.

Here's what I've learned:
Aligned partnerships are powerful. When you link arms with people who carry the same heart for impact, your capacity multiplies, and so does your reach.

Look for Partners Who:

- **Share your values** and mission, not just your niche
- **Serve your same audience** in a way that complements your work
- Bring **mutual benefit** to the table—this isn't just about exposure, it's about growth on both sides

Ways to Collaborate:

- **Co-host a live session** or virtual training together
- Do **podcast interviews** or **Instagram Live swaps** to introduce each other to new audiences
- **Bundle products, services, or digital resources** to offer more value
- **Host a challenge, summit, or multi-speaker event** to build collective impact
- Invite guest experts into your **membership, course, or community**

And don't underestimate the power of *simple support*. Sometimes a thoughtful shoutout, referral, or DM can be the beginning of something significant.

Nurture the Relationship, Not Just the Result

Don't just network, **nurture**. The best partnerships are built on trust, not transaction. Take time to learn about the person, their mission, and their audience. Make space for genuine conversation and shared vision. When trust is the foundation, impact and growth will always follow.

Action Steps:

1. **Create or update** your lead magnet and launch a simple welcome email series
2. **Choose one tool** you'll commit to learning or integrating this month to streamline your systems
3. **Reach out to one potential collaborator—** someone whose message and mission align with yours.

Next Up:

Now that your systems are strong and your brand is growing with grace, we're going to talk about **scaling without burnout**—because the goal isn't just to grow bigger, it's to grow better.

Affirmation:

I give myself permission to grow with grace.
I build systems that support my purpose and
protect my peace.

Chapter Ten

Scaling Impact Without Burnout

"Every good and perfect gift is from above, coming down from the Father of lights..."
—James 1:17

Growth is a blessing. Every new opportunity, every open door, every expansion of your reach is evidence of God's goodness in motion. But let's be clear—just because something is growing doesn't mean it's healthy. And just because it's a good thing doesn't mean it was meant for you to carry alone.

James 1:17 reminds us that every good and perfect gift is from above. That means your gifts, your ideas, your ability to serve and make an impact—they all come from God. But they weren't meant to drive you into exhaustion. You don't have to burn out to be effective. You don't have to lose yourself to be impactful.

This chapter is a reminder that your purpose is a gift. And if it's truly from God, it won't require you to sacrifice your well-being in order to fulfill it.

Let's talk about how to grow in a way that's sustainable, soulful, and strategic—without running yourself into the ground.

1. Recognizing Your Capacity

Before you add more to your plate, get honest about what's already there.

We live in a culture that glorifies hustle and praises productivity. But wise growth starts with awareness. You need to know your rhythms, your limits, your responsibilities, and what you truly have the capacity for.

When I first started my publishing company, it was just me and one client. Then I launched my first podcast. That podcast gave me a platform to connect with more authors. Eventually, those connections turned into more clients. Things picked up. Money was coming in. From the outside, it looked like everything was falling into place. But inside, I was overwhelmed. I didn't stop to pause and really evaluate what I could handle.

Full transparency—it led me to drop the ball more than once, not because I didn't care, but because my load was too heavy.

Most people won't tell you the behind-the-scenes of what building something really looks like. But if we're going to talk about owning your impact, we have to be real about what happens in the process.

Here's how you can check in with yourself while you grow:

Audit your energy
What drains you consistently? What gives you life? Pay attention to what leaves you feeling depleted versus what lights you up. This includes conversations, work tasks, and even people. If you want to impact others, be intentional about the impact others are having on you.

Understand your bandwidth
You can be passionate and still be tired. You can be

capable and still be overstretched. Take an honest inventory of your time, your mental and emotional energy, and the support system you have available. Be real about what this current season can hold.

Say no to good things
Just because it looks like an opportunity doesn't mean it's meant for you. Every yes should support your mission or protect your well-being. Period.

Just because you can carry it doesn't mean you're supposed to.

2. Building a Support Team or Community

You weren't designed to do it all. And you don't have to do it alone.

One of the best decisions you can make is to ask for help. That can be professional help or spiritual support—either way, it's necessary.

Here are a few ways to lighten your load without compromising your mission:

Hire a Virtual Assistant
Let someone else handle the routine stuff—emails, scheduling, social media, admin work. It's not about being too good for the small tasks. It's about freeing yourself up to stay focused on what only you can do.

Join a mastermind or find an accountability partner
You need people who get it. People who will challenge your excuses, remind you of your why, and hold you to

your goals. I can honestly say this has saved me during some of my busiest seasons.

Recruit volunteers or interns
If your brand has a clear mission or community focus, people will want to be a part of it. You can invite others in—ambassadors, beta readers, event helpers—and let them be part of your impact story too.

Stay plugged into your faith or wellness community
This is crucial. Whether it's church, small group, a coffee date with a friend, or a weekly check-in call with someone who truly sees you, you need people in your life who remind you of what matters most.

Your vision shouldn't cost you your peace. Let others help carry what you've been called to steward.

3. Staying Aligned as You Expand

Growth doesn't have to mean chaos. It can be intentional. It can be strategic. It can be rooted in what really matters.

The temptation when momentum builds is to say yes to everything. But more isn't always better. Sometimes more is just noise.

Here's how to stay aligned as you scale:

Go back to your "why"
Let your mission be the filter. Is this new opportunity aligned with what you were called to do? Is it still serving the people you're meant to help?

Pause before you pivot
You don't have to jump at every trend or opportunity. Give yourself time to discern. Sometimes clarity comes not from more movement, but from stillness.

Keep your messaging clear
As your offers grow, your voice should grow stronger— not more scattered. Make sure your audience still knows who you are, what you do, and why it matters.

Protect your boundaries
Your rest, your creativity, your values—these things must be guarded. As your brand grows, your boundaries should grow too.

You don't just want to grow. You want to grow well.

If your impact is leaving you empty, it's time to reassess. Not the vision, but the way you're carrying it.

James 1:17 reminds us that every good and perfect gift is from above. That includes your purpose. That includes your platform. That includes your pace.

You don't have to do more to be more. You don't have to exhaust yourself to be effective.

Let your growth reflect God's goodness—not your grind. Stay anchored in grace. Scale with intention. And above all else, protect the peace that God gave you when He gave you the gift.

You were never meant to do this alone.

Action Steps:

1. **Evaluate your current capacity.**
   How are you doing—emotionally, mentally, and physically? Are you stretched too thin or struggling silently? Write it down.
2. **Identify where support is needed.**
   What's one task, responsibility, or area that's weighing you down? Where could help make the biggest difference?
3. **Revisit your mission and vision.**
   Look at what you've added in the past 6–12 months. Is everything still aligned? Is anything stealing your peace or diluting your message?

Next Up:

In **Chapter 11**, we will talk about **Leading with Integrity and Faith**—because true leadership isn't just about what you build, but how you build it and *who you become* in the process.

Affirmation:

I protect my peace while I pursue purpose.
I ask for help when I need it and trust that support is part of the strategy.
I lead with wisdom, not overwhelm.

PART 4:

LEGACY + LONGEVITY

Chapter Eleven:

Leading with Integrity and Faith

As your influence grows, so will the pressure—to perform, to impress, to conform. But you weren't called to build your brand by blending in. You were called to stand out by standing firm.

This chapter is your reminder that real leadership is anchored in integrity. It flows from faith, not fear. It is less about chasing the spotlight and more about serving faithfully from the secret place.

1. Making Decisions Rooted in Values

Success is sweet, but peace is sacred.

Not every opportunity that glitters is aligned with your purpose. You must lead with discernment, not desperation.

Tips to Stay Aligned:

- **Anchor your goals in your "why."** When your goals reflect your values, you don't have to chase what everyone else is doing.
- **Run every yes through a values filter.** Ask: "Does this align with who I am and what I'm called to do?"
- **Use spiritual discernment.** Every open door isn't a divine one. Some things look like blessings but come with strings that pull you away from purpose.

"If it costs you your integrity, it's too expensive."

2. Showing Up Consistently Through Seasons

Faithful impact isn't about showing up perfect—it's about showing up present.

Life brings seasons. Some will overflow, others will stretch you thin. But when you commit to leading with grace, your consistency becomes your credibility.

How to Lead in Any Season:

- **In seasons of abundance:** Stay grounded and give God the glory.
- **In seasons of waiting:** Trust the process and keep serving behind the scenes.
- **In seasons of transition:** Lean on your foundation. Don't force the next—flow with it.

Your audience doesn't need constant perfection—they need your steady presence. They need to know that even leaders grow, wrestle, rest, and rise again.

Let your consistency reflect your **commitment**, not your **circumstances**.

3. Impact Over Image: Staying Grounded

The world rewards performance. God honors authenticity.

Real impact is built in the quiet moments—when you choose truth over trends, purpose over popularity, and character over convenience.

To Stay Grounded:

- **Choose authenticity over aesthetics.** It's okay if your journey isn't "curated." It's more powerful when it's *real*.
- **Prioritize legacy over likes.** Ask yourself, "What will people remember because I showed up?"
- **Lead from service, not ego.** The goal isn't to be admired—it's to make a difference.

Stay rooted by:

- Remaining in **community and accountability**
- Nurturing your **spiritual life**
- Creating space for regular **reflection and prayer**

Your integrity will take you where charisma can't keep you.

Your greatest impact won't come from how loudly the world claps—it will come from how deeply lives are changed because you stayed the course.

You've been equipped with strategies, tools, and systems.

But above all, you've been called.

Action Steps: Walking It Out with Integrity and Faith

1. **Create a Values Filter for Decision-Making**
   Write down your top five core values and keep them visible in your workspace. Before accepting any opportunity or collaboration, ask: *"Does this align with my values and calling?"* Use this filter as a guide to protect your peace and purpose.
2. **Commit to a Consistency Practice**
   Choose one habit that reflects faithful leadership—whether it's a weekly check-in with your audience, a morning devotional, or journaling through your leadership journey. Stick with it for the next 30 days, regardless of your current season.
3. **Schedule a Monthly Reflection and Reset**
   Block out time each month for honest reflection and prayer. Use this time to assess whether your impact is still rooted in authenticity, service, and faith. Ask God to reveal any areas where image has crept in over integrity—and make adjustments accordingly.

Lead boldly. Lead faithfully. Lead with integrity.

You don't just carry influence—you carry light.

Affirmation:

I show up consistently, embracing every season with grace.
I choose impact over image, authenticity over approval.

Chapter Twelve

The Legacy You're Leaving

Every post, every book, every product, every conversation, it's not just about now. It's about what lasts. Your legacy is already being written. This chapter is your reminder that your impact isn't just about today's results, it's about the ripple effect you create for tomorrow.

1. Reflecting on Your Why Before you build more, look back at what started it all.

   • What ignited your desire to write, speak, or lead?
   • Who did you want to help?

   • What did you feel called to change? Go back to that original fire—and let it fuel your future. Legacy starts when you align your work with your why.

2. Turning Influence Into Legacy Likes fade. Trends shift. But the heart behind your work is what lives on.

   • Focus on transformation, not just visibility.

   • Think generationally: How will your work serve others five, ten, twenty years from now?

   • Build assets that last: books, teachings, systems, and values that people can grow from long after you're gone. Legacy is not ego—it's impact with eternal purpose.

3. Inspiring Others to Own Their Impact Too You've walked the journey. Now be the proof that it's possible.

   • Mentor someone coming behind you.

   • Share your story boldly and without shame.

   • Lead in a way that gives others permission to show up, too. When you own your impact, you empower others to own theirs.

The Shift in My Business

There's a shift happening in my business, one I feel led to share with you.

For years, I've poured my heart into publishing, helping authors bring their stories to life through my imprint. I'm deeply proud of that work. It's sacred, and it has shaped so much of who I am.

But lately, I've felt a pull. Not to walk away from publishing, but to expand the vision. To step back from solely producing books and step into a new lane: equipping other publishers and publishing consultants to build thriving, impactful companies of their own.

And just as important, I'm leaning into deeper connection.
More live classes.
More coaching.
More honest conversations about purpose, obedience, and showing up when it's hard.

I've always felt a deep pull to help others build what God created them to build. I'm a true purpose pusher at heart.

I know how exhausting building a business can be—chasing down unpaid invoices, trying to network, spreading the word, all while managing the behind-the-scenes chaos no one else sees. It can feel like you're giving everything and still falling short.

That's why my impact is rooted in this: helping others make an impact without burning out.

Because purpose was never meant to drain you. It was meant to fuel you.

Here's the truth: writing a book isn't just about checking it off a list. It's about who you become in the process.

I want to help others not only publish but rise—walk boldly in their calling, build brands rooted in clarity, and create lasting impact for the people they're called to serve.

This shift doesn't erase where I've been. It honors it. And it creates space for what's next.

Legacy Challenge:
Take a moment to reflect and write your own legacy letter or personal mission statement. Start with one of these prompts:
"I want my life's work to stand for…"
"The impact I want to leave behind is…"
"Those I hope to inspire are…"

Let this guide how you move forward.

You are more than an author. More than an entrepreneur. You are a change agent. A leader. A light. A legacy in motion.

The world needs what's in you.

Conclusion: Your Impact Journey Starts Now

You've made it to the final pages, but this isn't the end. It's the beginning of your next level. You've explored how to own your story, elevate your voice, and build something that matters. Now it's time to take action, not just inspiration. Whether you're just getting started or shifting into a new season, know this: You are called. You are capable. And your impact matters.

Encouragement to Take the Next Step

Don't wait for perfect timing. Don't wait to feel "ready." Start with what you have. Use what you know. Show up imperfectly but intentionally. The next chapter of your journey is waiting—and it's one only you can write.

Reflection Questions:

Take a moment to sit with what this journey has stirred in you:

1. What is one belief about yourself or your work that has shifted after reading this book?
2. What does "owning your impact" mean to you right now?
3. What is one action you will take this week to walk in your purpose?
4. Who can you support, serve, or encourage as they step into their impact?
5. What does legacy look like in your life and business?

Stay Connected

Your impact journey is personal—but you don't have to do it alone.

I'd love to stay connected and support you as you continue growing in purpose and influence:

- **Website**: Grace4purposeco.com
- **Join the Impact Community**: https://theauthorsimpacthub.com/the-authors-impact-hub
- **Connect on Social**:

  Instagram:
  @_juanitanicole_
  @authorsimpacthub
  @m4mlegacyunlocked

  Facebook:

  Juanita Nicole Woodson
  Authors Impact Hub
  Moments for Moms: Legacy Unlocked

- **Listen to the Podcast**:

  Authors Impact Hub Podcast
  Hope at the End of The Tunnel Podcast

You're not just a reader, you're part of a movement.
A movement of purpose-driven authors, entrepreneurs, and leaders changing lives one step at a time.

Now go.....**own your impact!**

About the Author

Juanita N. Woodson, a devoted wife and nurturing mother, stands as a beacon of inspiration in both her personal and professional life. As a best-selling author, skillfully woven her testimony into books that captivate the hearts and minds of readers around the world.

In addition to her literary accomplishments, Juanita is the visionary owner of Grace 4 Purpose Publishing Co. LLC. With a passion for empowering others, she dedicates her time to coaching aspiring authors, guiding them on their journey to not only write but also successfully publish their own stories. Her commitment to nurturing the creative spirit within each individual is reflected in the diverse and impactful works that emerge under her guidance.

Beyond the realm of publishing, Juanita is a multifaceted entrepreneur who seamlessly balances the roles of mentor, leader, and advocate. Her dedication to the written word is matched only by her commitment to fostering a community where aspiring writers can flourish and find their voices.

In her quest to leave an indelible mark on the literary landscape, Juanita N. Woodson continues to inspire, uplift, and empower those around her, leaving an enduring legacy of creativity, resilience, and purpose.

Own Your Impact

Other Books

Don't Go That Way: Protect Your Purpose

My Comfort Zone is Broken

Put it Down: Gentle Reminders for Healing

Moments for Moms Volume I: Give Yourself a Minute Mama

Moments for Moms Volume II: Peace, Patience, and Balance

Moments for Moms III: Journeys of Joy & Resilience

Faith While Waiting Volume I

Resources

Ready to launch your podcast with confidence and clarity?

Book your Comprehensive Podcast Training Coaching Session today and let me help you map out your content, develop your voice, and get your show into the ears of the people who need your message.

SCAN TO BOOK

Own Your Impact

Leave a Review